UK UFOs

Alan Toner

Copyright © 2016 Alan Toner

All rights reserved. No part of this publication can be reproduced or transmitted in any form or by any means without permission in writing from the Author.

ISBN-13: 978-1537645834
ISBN-10: 1537645838

Other Books by Alan Toner

True Ghost Stories
True Ghost Stories 2
Famous Psychics
Hammer Horror Remembered
Werewolf Nightmare

Contents

Chapter One: Rendlesham Forest UFO.................................1
Chapter Two: The Dudley Durito...6
Chapter Three: The Bexley Heath UFOs...............................9
Chapter Four: The Ilkley Moor Alien..................................11
Chapter Five: RAF Cosford & Shawbury Incident 14
Chapter Six: The Bonsall UFO Video................................17
Chapter Seven: The British UFO Research Association....19
Chapter Eight: The Cornwall UFO Triangle......................22
Chapter Nine: Kent, The UFO Hotspot..............................24
Chapter Ten: Merseyside UFOs...27
Chapter Eleven: UFOs Over London.................................32
Author's Note..34

Chapter One: Rendlesham Forest UFO

They called it Britain's Roswell. However, in reality, the Rendlesham Forest UFO incident held much more significance than its American counterpart, and is in fact one of the most famous cases ever recorded in the annals of British UFO history.

Did an alien spacecraft land in this Suffolk forest in the winter of 1980?

Although the whole case is shrouded in secrecy and complexity (with the passage of years, the facts surrounding the incident have become increasingly nebulous, as statements alter and new witnesses speak out), the main features that characterised the Rendlesham Forest UFO incident are quite clear and familiar, and are as follows.

On December 26th 1980, around 3.00 a.m., a couple of security guards, posted near the east gate of RAF Woodbridge, observed bright lights apparently descending into Rendlesham Forest. Simultaneously, a bright fireball burned up over southern England.

The guards went out into the forest and saw a strange light flashing between the trees. When they began to follow it, they discovered that its source was a lighthouse called Orford Ness.

As dawn broke, a number of indentations in the ground and marks on the trees were found in a clearing. Carefully examining them, a forester and local police identified these as rabbit scrapings and cuts made by foresters.

Two nights later, a different rank of military personnel – namely the deputy base commander, Lt Col Charles Halt – experienced a similar string of mysterious happenings. A rather pragmatic person who wanted to disprove the wild rumours coming from RAF bases Woodbridge and Bentwaters, Halt, armed with a recording device, conducted a thorough investigation of the area. The resulting audiotape is now deemed to be one of the most valuable, fascinating items of evidence in the Rendlesham Forest incident.

Halt also took some radiation readings, which were background levels. He also spotted a flashing light in the direction of Orford Ness. However, he was unable to identify it.

Col Halt also reported seeing strange objects that twinkled and hovered around for quite a few hours, objects that looked like stars, the brightest of which was in the direction of Sirius. This star occasionally seemed to send down strange beams of light.

The transcript of Halt's audio tape runs to some 18 minutes in length, and includes statements from Halt as he describes, in lurid, compelling detail, all that he witnessed during his investigation in the forest. In subsequent interviews, Halt claims that these occurrences were registered by British radar.

The following night, December 28, yet another group of men claim to have witnessed something extremely odd in Rendlesham Forest. Larry Warren, an 18-year-old soldier, was sent out on patrol with Sgt Adrian Bustinza and a few other military personnel. Sometime after 11pm, the men departed their trucks and made for the field where lights had been spotted on the previous two nights. In this location, Warren claims to have seen disaster preparedness officers with geiger counters, walking slowly around an object on the ground, studying it closely. A small red light was then seen approaching from the direction of the coast. The light, Warren claims, moved in a downward arc, so fast it stopped and hovered about 20 feet off the ground. Warren describes it as "the size of an American basketball." He also claims it was "self-illuminated, not quite red." And it was then that events took an even weirder turn.

The red light suddenly exploded, and a craft appeared on the forest floor. Warren describes this craft as having "no windows, no markings, no flag or country of origin. Nothing." Warren also claims that you could not stare straight at the object, and that if you looked at it through the periphery of your vision, you'd perceive its general shape, a shape as clear as crystal. Could this shape have been that of some extra terrestrial spacecraft that had encroached on the earth's airspace?

Warren and Bustinza were then asked to back off by a senior official. Watching from a distance, they then claim to have witnessed Wing Commander Gordon Williams approach the craft and confront some kind of alien being. They describe the being as having what looked like eyes, some facial features, bright clothing and holding some kind of device (a weapon, perhaps?). Warren is adamant that a silent exchange, rather than any actual verbal communication, took place.

When Warren returned to his base around 4.30 am, Bustinza claims to have seen the craft depart. He described the craft as "hovering," ascending at a 45-degree angle, and going so fast that to blink would have missed it. Bustinza also describes experiencing a "cold draft of air," akin to a strong gust of wind or dust, which lasted for around ten seconds.

It is believed that nearly half of all UFO correspondence sent to the Ministry of Defence pertains to the Rendlesham

Alan Toner

Forest incident. Although there have been claims of a cover up, the MoD have always maintained that there was no evidence to suggest of any major threat to the United Kingdom, either from extra terrestrials or otherwise. But that is not what Daniel Simpson, director of the Rendlesham UFO Incident (a fictionalised account of the case set in modern-day Rendlesham Forest) believes. Simpson is convinced that either there has indeed been a military cover-up, or that something very significant connected with aliens occurred in December 1980. He also claims to have actual evidence to substantiate his claims, which he came about when he was filming in Rendlesham Forest. He discovered a series of mysterious hatches in the forest, and called on the Forestry Commission to investigate.

When the Commission's investigators towed off one of the hatches with a four-wheel drive, they discovered a ladder going down to a very elaborate drainage system. Simpson believes that the RAF bases of Woodbridge and Bentwaters are connected by a network of tunnels running underneath. And he tells an interesting story of a guy who went up to the Bentwaters air base to sort out an Internet connection for some local people living on the base. When the guy returned, his face was as white as a sheet, for he'd stumbled on something very curious there. What he'd seen were cables two foot down, and delivering an exceptionally powerful Internet connection. But the strange thing was, these cables dated back to 1980, long before the days of powerful Internet connections!

Simpson is uncertain as to whether this really is a military cover-up, or whether it is something more disturbing. He is, however, convinced that something very strange occurred in Rendlesham Forest all those years ago, and is certainly not hesitant in attributing the incident to possible alien activity.

In essence, the Rendlesham Forest UFO Incident boils down to the misinterpretation of a series of nocturnal lights: a lighthouse, a fireball, and some stars. Such misidentifications are common in the world of UFO investigation. It is only the link of three different stimuli that differentiates it and makes it so remarkable.

Despite the opinions of many blinkered sceptics, Rendlesham is one of the few undisputed UFO close encounter events ever recorded. It is quite unique, for it wasn't just witnessed by the proverbial dog-walker or a couple of drunks staggering home from the pub, but an entire team of experienced and level-headed USAF personnel, many of whom have provided detailed first hand accounts. Therefore, it might be wise to point out to those who are inclined to scoff at such things to familiarise themselves fully with the case before being so quick to debunk it.

The Rendlesham Forest incident continues to fascinate UFO enthusiasts and conspiracy theorists the world over, and it's very easy to understand why. There have also been a number of books on the case, the most recent being Encounter In Rendlesham Forest by Nick Pope and John Burroughs.

Chapter Two: The Dudley Durito

The Dudley Durito is the name given to a string of UFO sightings in the form of black triangular craft, spotted hovering over the West Midlands conurbation area of the United Kingdom since 2007. Different people claimed to have seen these strange objects, and one family claims to have even captured them on video.

The first Dudley Durito sighting occurred on the 28th November 2007. A witness saw the object hovering initially over Halesowen, Dudley, before moving on in the direction of Stourbridge. Around the same time, another witness from the Lickey Hills area saw a similar object flying, at great speed, through the Birmingham horizon whilst they were exploring the locality with their binoculars.

When the sightings were reported to local UFO study group UFORM, they released a statement to the local press, quoting one of the witnesses who described the object resembling a "huge Dorito and had distinctive red lights on its underside, which moved position while the craft was flying." This description gave rise to the local press dubbing the object 'The Dudley Dorito'.

An object of similar description was seen by people around the Dudley, Wednesbury and Bushbury areas of the West Midlands, between 4.00 pm and 7.30 pm, on the same day as the first sighting. They described the object as large, triangular in shape, with three lights at each corner, and silent. The triangular object was also spotted over Quinton in late November, and it was filmed by a senior member of a local UFO group. The object was described as huge and displaying three red lights.

The triangular object was also witnessed by two young girls, aged

UK UFOs

7 and 9, on Tuesday, 8th January 2008, when they were staying over at their grandmother's house in Dudley. Alarmed by what they saw, the two girls flew out of bed and ran to their grandmother. After hearing their story, she made them draw pictures of what they had seen. The girls drew a diamond in the shape of an isosceles triangle. One drew the object with three lights, the other with four. Their story was given further weight by members of the public, who had also witnessed the strange UFO and described it as an arrowhead shape displaying three orange lights. Furthermore, Birmingham International stated they had also received similar reports of this object, and were now treating the matter extremely seriously.

At 4.10 pm on Monday, 4th January 2008, a sonic boom attributed to an RAF Eurofighter Typhoon was heard in the Shropshire area. As a result, local radio stations were flooded with calls by people claiming that they had seen two large aircraft in the area. Simultaneously, there were reports that a Eurofighter had suffered an unknown malfunction, resulting in a 30,000ft plunge and causing a sonic boom, which shook the whole county. However, both nearby RAF Shawbury and the Ministry of Defence denied any links to his occurrence. The local press compared descriptions of the unidentified object and that of the Eurofighter, and suggested that there was a link to the sightings due to their similarities.

In 2011, the Dudley Durito made yet another appearance, this time turning up around a Midlands beauty spot. A property worker, Gary Nock, and his family were standing on the car park of the Badgers Sett pub, Hagley, around 6.40 pm, when they suddenly spotted the distinctive object flying overhead. Nock, 52, described the UFO as being triangular in shape, with white lights at each end, and flying at low altitude. It had seemed to come from the direction of Birmingham. Nock said that the object then seemed to turn silently in the air, before fading out of site as it flew over the Clent Hills.

As soon as he got back home, Nock looked it up on the Internet. He said the UFO bore a close resemblance to the "Dudley Dorito", first spotted over the skies of the Black Country a few years ago. Mr Nock said there was a possibility that the craft could have been an experimental military aircraft, like a B2 stealth plane. However, such a plane tends to make a distinctive sound, unlike the object that Nock saw, which was eerily silent. Nock also said that he had never seen anything like this before. The sighting thus totally mystified Mr Nock and his family.

The mysterious triangular shaped object known as the "Dudley Durito" has since spotted by a security officer while he was in the back garden of his home, plus by many other witnesses in the Tipton, Brierley Hill and Oldbury areas. As well as being described as triangular, the object has also been compared to a "flying crisp".

Chapter Three: The Bexley Heath UFOs

On July 17th, 1955, a lady by the name of Margaret Fry was making her way to her doctor's surgery in King Harold's Way from her house in Hythe Avenue, Bexley Heath, when she suddenly spotted a strange object hovering in the sky. She wasn't the only one who saw this object, for it was also witnessed by her doctor and around a dozen local children who were playing in the street.

Mrs Fry described the object as "saucer-shaped, with a "blue/silver/grey/pewter texture, yet none of those colours." She also said it had three spheres set into its base, one of which "flopped out", landing on the ground at the junction of nearby Ashbourne and Whitfield Roads.

When the children cautiously approached the object for a closer look, it suddenly rose back up into the sky and vanished from view after a few minutes.

Rodney Maynard, who was just 15 at the time, recalls the incident very clearly. Working as a labourer on a building site in nearby Streamway, he was just taking his lunch break with his workmates when word got back to them that something very odd was happening in King Harold's Way. When Rodney and his colleagues rushed there to investigate, they saw that the object had landed in the road, taking up the whole width of it and overlapping onto the pavements. The craft wasn't actually sitting on the ground, but floating a few feet above it. Fascinated observers who had all gathered round the craft to watch it heard a strange humming sound emitting from its metallic body. The craft had around eight huge suckers, and the centre was unmoving, but the outer rim was spinning slowly. It also had white lights flashing, in a manner akin to a camera flash. Rodney also recalls that the craft had what appeared to be windows, although the glass was concave in shape and moulded together, so that nothing inside was discernible.

As a couple of the crowd ventured forward to touch the craft, it began to spin faster and faster. It then began to ascend slowly, tilting lightly, and then hovering over their heads. It then moved slowly until it was over Bedonwell Primary School, where it hovered again for around a minute. It then shot up into the sky and vanished.

Rodney says that his brother, 16 at the time, also witnessed the craft, which was described as "black, sleek and streamlined, with a surface like polished metal". Rodney maintains to this day that what he saw was definitely not some kind of manufactured joke, and has never forgotten it. He is, however, rather reluctant to talk about it too much for fear of being regarded as a crazy tall-story teller. Even his own mother took a very dim view of him broaching the subject, as was the case with the parents of all his friends, who also witnessed the mysterious craft.

As for Mrs Fry, she is now in her late 70s and lives in Abergele, North Wales. She recounts her experience in a book called Who Are They? She also talks about other UFO sightings in the Kent and Bexley areas, and has been helping UFO enthusiast and retired policeman John Hanson with his own books on the subject.

Chapter Four: The Ilkley Moor Alien

The Ilkley Moor, in Yorkshire, England, has a setting very similar to that of the moors surrounding Baskerville Hall, the location in Conan Doyle's Sherlock Holmes story, 'The Hound of the Baskervilles'. It's a barren landscape of mud, rock, swamp, and prehistoric cairn stones. It has a very creepy atmosphere, especially at night. It is also a place of mystery, and has the following landmarks: the Swastika stone; boulders etched with strange markings; the Badger Stone; and the Twelve Apostles stone circle. It is also the centre of a rather unique case of alien abduction, which occurred on 1st December 1987.

In the early morning of that day, a former policeman named Philip Spencer was walking southward across Ilkley Moor, equipped with a compass for navigation and a camera (it was his intention to catch, on film, some of the strange anomalies that the eerie moor is noted for, while on the way to visit his father-in-law in East Morton). He soon found himself surrounded by a cold, damp, Yorkshire fog. Then, through a parting of this mist - which almost seemed to have a life of its own - he allegedly first glimpsed what looked to be an alien being. This strange figure then started waving at him, as if gesturing for him to go away. Spencer quickly snapped the being with his camera. As if startled, the creature swiftly moved out of sight.

Some moments later, it was Spencer's turn to be startled, as an unidentifiable craft resembling two saucers stuck top to bottom, with a domed top, lifted off from behind an outcrop and, emitting a loud humming sound, disappeared into the clouds.

Utterly confused and wondering if he was going mad, Spencer decided to cancel the visit to his in-laws and head instead for the nearby village of Menston. On the way, he noticed the needle on his compass now pointed south instead of north. Also, when he arrived at his destination, he noticed that the church clock showed the time as 10:00 a.m., not 8:15 a.m., which was the time it should have been.

Spencer then made his way to Keighley to get the film in his camera developed. When the process was completed, the picture appeared to show an image of a four-foot being with very long arms and bluish-green skin. When Kodak Laboratories analysed the picture, they concluded that it had not been tampered with in any way. The photo was then sent to the United States and, when it was computer enhanced, the results proved inconclusive.

In the aftermath of his strange experience, Spencer started to have weird dreams. After contacting UFO investigator Peter Hough, he consented to having regressive hypnosis, and this revealed that he had been abducted, subjected to some kind of examination, given a tour of the spacecraft, and taken on a journey into outer space. He was then given some videos to view by his alien captors. The first video seemed to warn of a future world catastrophe, but the second video he was forbidden to discuss. When Spencer was finally returned to the moor unharmed, the snapshot he had in his possession depicted the alien waving goodbye.

Some sceptics may regard Spencer's whole experience as just one big hoax. However, they should remember that he was a policeman and, as such, had a credible, solid background. Moreover, his story has never changed over time.

UK UFOs

Spencer never received any financial gain from either the story or the picture, as all the copyright privileges were signed over to Peter Hough.

Chapter Five: RAF Cosford & Shawbury Incident

In late March 1993, there was a mass UFO sighting in the UK that became known as the "Cosford Incident", or the "British UFO Mystery".

Somerset was the location of the first sighting, which occurred around 8.30 pm on 30th March. There was a further sighting in Quantock Hills at 9.00 pm. Both sightings resulted in hundreds of reports flooding into the MoD and local police stations, most of which were filed. In addition, many more people from all walks of life witnessed the UFO, but did not feel inclined to report it to the authorities. Most of the reports described the object as "triangular" in shape, displaying white lights at each point which swept back and forth.

According to the reports, many people saw the strange craft at very close range, within 200 - 400 feet from the ground. One family in Staffordshire saw the object hovering so low to the ground that, at first, they thought it had landed in a field. They instantly raced to the suspected landing site in their car, but when they got there, they could find no trace of the object. They did, however, describe how they heard a strange, low, humming sound. And not only did they hear it, but they claim they actually felt it as well. They say the sensation was very akin to standing in front of a bass speaker.

When the UFO then flew over two military bases - RAF Cosford and RAF Shawbury - at least three people on guard patrol at the latter base saw it. They immediately filed reports, which is the

UK UFOs

normal procedure whenever anything unidentified is spotted flying over any military base. A check of the radar revealed that there was nothing scheduled to fly that night anywhere near the bases. A thorough investigation was then launched into the potential radar findings and, strangely enough, one of the primary radar heads was either intentionally disabled or had been disabled prior to the UFO appearance, thus rendering any possible radar information inconclusive.

A meteorologist at RAF Shawbury also witnessed the UFO whilst preparing for the next day's weather report. He was completely awestruck to see a solid object in the sky. He described the object as a craft around 200 feet long, and said it looked like a cross between Hercules C-130 Military Transport plane and a 747 flying directly over the RAF Shawbury. He also heard the low humming sound emitting from the craft.

The meteorologist also claimed that the craft was radiating a beam of light towards a field just beyond the perimeter of the base fence. The light was sweeping back and forth, as if attempting to detect something on the ground. Eventually the beam of light retracted and the craft moved off. Apparently, the craft was moving at a speed of between 20 -40 mph. Several civilian witnesses verified the meteorologist's story.

Most sceptics, however, have suggested rather less sensational explanations. On the evening of March 30, 1993, Russia launched a radio satellite into orbit. The rocket booster, which took it into space, later re-entered the earth's atmosphere, breaking into a few pieces as it did so. All of the sightings of 'bright lights' coincide with a computer simulation of where the fragments would have been visible.

And meteorological officer Wayne Elliott, whose

Alan Toner

evidence at Shawbury was central, has pointed out that his sighting occurred an hour after the one at Cosford – and he now believes what he saw was actually just a police helicopter.

Chapter Six: The Bonsall UFO Video

The Bonsall UFO incident occurred in Bonsall, Derbyshire, near Matlock, on October 5th 2000. A woman named Sharon Rowlands, a resident of Slaley, claims to have seen a large luminous object, with a shimmering pink colour, hovering and rotating over a nearby field.

Responding to an eerie noise outside her home on that October evening, she filmed quite a bit of the object's activity on a camcorder. The video shows an out-of-focus ball of light that looks to be made out of concentric circles very similar to that of a photographic orb. The object resembled a giant disc with a bite taken out of the bottom The video becomes slightly out-of-focus as she tries to zoom in closer to the object. Rowlands reported it to her local newspaper, the Matlock Mercury, which then published her story. Ms Rowlands was so convinced of the film's authenticity that she had locked it in a Nottingham bank vault before sending it to America.

The story soon attracted the interest of local UFO researchers, who recognized Rowlands object as being similar in appearance to an object observed in a video taken as part of the STS-75 Space Shuttle mission in February 1996. However, a NASA engineer has expressed his doubts about this claim, and opines that the object is one of the many occurrences of debris, dust, particles or optical aberrations that are noticeable in virtually every video of a shuttle mission. Careful analysis carried out by other organisations, such as

Project P.R.O.V.E., also give weight to this conclusion. Consequently, a number of UFO websites, which initially thought the video showed stark evidence of huge numbers of UFOs, have since withdrawn their claims.

The two videos have been subjected to intense scrutiny by UFO experts. They believe that the NASA video shows an object that is rotating and maintaining its geometric shape as it revolves, a fact that could rule out the possibility of a photographic deviation.

On Friday 1st June 2001, it was reported on the BBC News website that Sharon Rowlands sold her UFO video to a Hollywood producer. She was reportedly to have been paid £20,000 for the footage. Furthermore, NASA officials were said to have asked to examine the tape, believing it shows the same type of craft once observed by the space agency's own cameras during a space shuttle mission.

Ms Rowlands' experience is just one of many alleged sightings of strange objects in the sky over Bonsall during those few months. For example, one woman reported seeing a "ball of fire" in the skies, while another claimed she witnessed "two big, bright lights". Also, a man out walking his dog observed a "pink glow, vertically shaped like a shoe box".

The Meteorological Office said there were no anomalous weather conditions that might have explained Ms Rowland's sighting. Others attribute the sightings to military aircraft.

Chapter Seven: The British UFO Research Association

The British UFO Research Association (formerly known as the London UFO Research Organisation in 1959) was formed in 1962 from a coalition of British UFO societies. It was legally constituted in 1975 as a non-profit company, whose primary aim was to conduct in-depth research and investigation of UFO phenomenon in the British Isles. The organisation now has around 1000 members. Its current Director of Investigations is Heather Dixon.

In 1991, Major Sir Patrick Wall compiled the book UFO Encyclopedia for the group. However, there was a certain entry in this book, a sighting initially confirmed as genuine by BUFORA, which was later discovered to be a hoax. The supposed witness, who claimed to have seen a UFO hovering over the town of Warminster, admitted to the hoax in 1994. In 1995 the group were the only official UFO organisation to endorse a film, purportedly by the US government, showing an alien autopsy at Roswell.

Since the 1970s, the association has run a specialist training course in investigations. BUFORA also formed a code of practice for investigators, which continues into the present, with all reports lead by the witness in every case.

BUFORA investigates over 400 cases a year, with the organisation reporting 95% of them as hoaxes. They also run witness support groups for those who claim they have encountered aliens. The organisation has been holding an annual conference at Sheffield Hallam University since 1987, in addition to meetings

Alan Toner

across the country. Rendlesham Forest, once a scene of a major UFO sighting, is a frequent spot for gatherings.

BUFORA continues to be an important contributor and consultant to UFO news, reports, documentaries and articles over the years, with many well-respected UFO researchers as part of its team. Its 50th anniversary conference was staged in London in 2012.

Its official website is: www.bufora.org.uk/

Chapter Eight: The Cornwall UFO Triangle

According to the Cornwall UFO Research Group, Cornwall has the most UFO sightings and paranormal activity due to a "triangle" that exists in the county. This triangle of supposed alien activity stretches from Land's End to Falmouth Bay to St. Ives Bay.

A spokesman for the group says that it is very difficult - in fact, almost impossible - to acquire well balanced, objective data for both alleged UFO sightings and supernatural occurrences in the area. He also claims that calculations were based on first-hand experiences, actual on-site investigations, case studies, and various discussions with other Ufologists. He said that when many different types of reported psychic, paranormal and anomalous phenomena are put together and given the same statistical assessing, three localities appear to stand out: Cornwall, Norfolk and an area bounded by Harrogate, York and Leeds.

A survey conducted in the area concluded that there have been more than 60 UFO sightings in Cornwall, compared to a national average of 40 sightings for comparable areas.

The most recent sighting of a UFO in the Cornwall Triangle area occurred on the 17th February 2015, when a mysterious object was photographed in the airspace above Cornwall around the time that RAF jet fighters were summoned to intercept two Russian bombers that were observed flying near the coast. This UFO was reported to be triangular in shape, and was seen hovering over people on Summerleaze Beach, Bude. An unknown person took the snap and

UK UFOs

sent it to the Cornwall UFO Research Group, who posted it on their social media sites the following day. This immediately generated much concern and confusion, as that was the same day that the Russian bombers were spotted over the coast. Although some reports said that the planes flew inland, this was disputed by the Ministry of Defence.

But that wasn't the end of the incident, for the Cornwall UFO Research Group received a second picture from another person, this one depicting a different UFO flying over Bude on February 3rd.

Different suggestions were made as to what the UFO could possibly be. One person thought it was a remote-controlled seagull a relative was playing with, but this is doubtful, taking into account the size and the fact that the object bears not the slightest resemblance to a remote-controlled seagull. There is also the theory that the UFOs are being so attracted to the Cornwall Triangle area due to its beautiful, pollution free skies. However, again, this suggestion has not really been proved as fact.

Chapter Nine: Kent, The UFO Hotspot

According to the National Archives, Dartford, Bromley and Forest Hill in Kent are very popular spots for UFOs to visit.

Bromley Hill, in particular, is said to be the "King of UFO sightings" in the South East, with some of the highest figures in the UK. For example, one incident in particular, which occurred in November 2003, attracted the attention of the Metropolitan Police. A family filmed around 30 red flashing lights in the sky, accompanied a chilling whirring noise. Both the police and even a Met helicopter witnessed this incident too. One police officer described the lights as making zigzagging movements, turning across the sky at a speed faster than any normal aircraft. When the Met asked the Ministry of Defence if radar tapes for the area showed anything unusual, they were informed that nothing strange had been detected, and that no aircraft were in the sky at the time.

On Valentine's Day in 1996, one Lewisham resident reported spotting a "round star-shaped object" that was stationary and very high in the sky. A year before, on July 7th, a shiny ball-shaped object was seen flying over the observer's residence, around 60ft from the ground.

In the early evening of April 20th 1995, in Beckenham, a number of people witnessed a sinister-looking, oval-shaped object hovering below the top level of a block of flats. The object was grey in colour, and moved swiftly and silently into the distance. Just two years later, another object was spotted shining brightly in the sky,

UK UFOs

this one displaying red, green and blue colouring, and moving in an easterly direction.

On August 3rd 1997, a large UFO was said to have alighted in the woods near Bexley. The official reports, however, reveal no further details on the uncanny event's exact location. Again in Bexley, in 2007, there were reports of around 50 strange lights. Orange and red in colour, some wondered if they were Chinese lanterns, or simply alien craft seeking out something lost.

On June 15th 1993, in Brockley, three triangular-shaped objects - red, white and black in colour - were reported flying alongside an aeroplane. They then shot ahead of the plane, coming together before seemingly vanishing into thin air. The strange incident lasted for about four minutes, and was also witnessed by somebody at John Stainer Primary School during dinnertime. Six years later, another Brockley resident observed an object shaped like a boomerang, flying silently across the sky and heading in a northeast direction.

In Orpington, on August 29th 1995, a silver metallic object, shaped like a dome, was spotted flying very high in the sky. The object displayed around 20 white lights, which turned red and orange. Again, on October 17th 2009, mysterious orange and red lights, trailing vapour, flew over the Orpington skyline. It eventually span off and disappeared in a flash of green and blue colours.

At the Dartford Crossing, there have been an exceptionally high number of UFO sightings. For example, in 1988, two strange objects were spotted. The first one was in March, in the form of a white balloon-shaped object that was observed moving slowly across the sky before vanishing. The second one occurred in December, when a triangular-shaped object with lights along its sides was spotted moving to the left and the west.

A driver in Hayes was almost scared witless in 1996 as he encountered something very strange on his journey. He reported being followed in his car by a large, silent, blue light, which hovered around 15ft off the ground. During the occurrence, the driver said he experienced a "time loss." Who knows what happened during those few lost minutes? Other sightings in the area include a very strange incident in 1988, when a small oblong-shaped object was reported in the northeast location, moving slowly and steadily across the sky. The object was described as being "very bright and silver" in appearance.

There have been many complaints from Forest Hill residents about possible alien activity plaguing their homes. For example, on May 24th 2001, one person reported an alien spacecraft near his home, which affected their electrical equipment. They described the craft as "disc-shaped, and emitting a beam of light." In another incident, a mysterious object sporting three green lights in a triangular formation was seen hovering over the observer's house before suddenly vanishing. The strange craft made a "screeching, humming sound" as it went.

Chapter Ten: Merseyside UFOs

As a born and bred Merseysider and author of this book, I have to say that I have never actually seen a UFO myself over Merseyside (or in any other part of the country, for that matter). However, according to many reports I have read over the years, a lot of my fellow Scousers apparently have. Here are just a few of those sightings.

One Sunday evening on May 25th 2009, a number of people reported seeing strange glowing lights moving slowly across the sky over Merseyside, between 10.30 p.m. and 11.00 p.m. The areas where these sightings occurred were Southport, South Liverpool, Ainsdale, Garston and Mossley Hill. One witness described these UFOs as looking like "fiery red balls." She also said that when planes flew past, the lights just "dimmed."

Other witnesses also reported seeing a strange object dropping from one of the lights, comparing it to a "plastic bag on fire." A resident in Allerton Road described the lights as "appearing similar to stars, but much brighter." He initially assumed they must be satellites, as their arc suggested an orbit, but he was surprised at the sheer speed and pace they were going as they glided across the sky. The lights were photographed by the Liverpool Echo.

When these strange lights were brought to the attention of the Ministry of Defence, they said that although it was nothing new for military planes to fly over Merseyside, it would not offer any theories as to the cause of the lights.

An air traffic services manager at Liverpool John Lennon Airport said that having checked the flight records, they were unable to connect the reports with any aircraft movements at Liverpool around the time the lights were spotted.

A local coastguard opined that any orange glow could be attributed to the annual Eta Aquarids meteor shower. Also, a Liverpool UFO expert said it was the norm that strange lights spotted in the sky usually turn out to be nothing more than floating Chinese lanterns.

In my hometown of Birkenhead, on the evening of the 3rd November 2009, a local man claimed to have sighted a UFO hovering over the town. Sitting having a smoke outside his home in Patterson Street, the man noticed a very strange light in the sky around 9.00 p.m. The light seemed to be coming down "really fast". Then it stopped, moved around somewhat, before starting to drop again. The man was positive it wasn't a firework or a maroon, as it seemed to move in very definite directions, as if it were being guided. He did manage to take a photograph of it and got some video for his mobile phone. However, the UFO then moved away for his line of sight and over the houses.

Again on the Wirral, one Friday night in August 1996, a local man, Colin, having just met up with his mate Steve (who was a chef) after he'd finished work, was taking his usual walk along the public footpath leading up to Bidston Golf Course, around 12.30 p.m., when he experienced something very strange. Upon reaching the golf course, both men were startled as they suddenly became engulfed by a thick fog. Then, as they both looked up, they saw a ball of light, shaped like an anchor, moving in a rather automated fashion. Although the light was high above the buildings, it was, at the same time, in close proximity to the men. Then they heard somebody - or something - running towards them, making a panting noise. They claimed it wasn't a dog, as they were well familiar with the sound that that animal makes. It sounded more like a human, and terrified the men. Then, as they ran towards the edge of the coarse, the thick fog disappeared.

It was a real warm summer's night, and so there shouldn't have been any mist or fog at all. Colin says that when he looked at Steve's watch, he noticed it was 1.30 p.m., which puzzled him immensely. Colin claims they arrived at the spot at around 12.30 p.m., yet what they experienced didn't last for a duration of 45 minutes; it must have lasted for 5 minutes at the most, a time discrepancy which, to this day, Colin still can't explain. Sadly, his mate, Steve, is no longer here to support Colin's story, as he passed away a few years ago. Colin is adamant that what they witnessed all those years ago on the briefly fog-shrouded Bidston Hill was definitely not a helicopter, as it would have dispersed the fog. Also, there was no engine sound. He is, therefore, still at a complete loss as to just exactly what that strange object was.

In Ellesmere Port, there have been many claims over the years that aliens have actually visited the area. A total of 30 UFOs were reported in the region over a 10-year period, two of which actually involved the town itself. For example, on Saturday 4th November 2009, seven to eight bright orange flame lights were spotted in the sky over Ellesmere Port. They were not thought to be a plane or helicopter, and they made no noise. The lights moved swiftly across the sky before disappearing.

Other reports on the Internet refer to a huge flash that lit up the sky in an orange and yellow glow in the Cheshire Oaks area, and exactly 20 orange balls moving in an east-west direction. Some of these balls moved at a faster pace than the others, as if they were trying to catch up to the main group.

In mid-January 2015, a UFO sighting was reported on Merseyside. A strange circular-shaped object, emitting a bright pulsating light, was spotted hovering very close to a residence in Formby. The witness (who is unnamed) observed the UFO outside their bedroom window, and said that the incident lasted for around 10 minutes. They described the object as resembling a "star", only bigger and bright white. Initially, the witness thought it was a plane, but subsequently realised that it couldn't have been, because the strange craft was in a stationary position. The incident occurred at 3.00 a.m. on Sunday, January 18th, on Crown Close, near Liverpool Road.

In 2013, a Merseyside family turned to the Government for help after claiming they were being terrified by aliens outside their home. The family members reported seeing three bright objects flying in the same direction near their house. They say the lights hovered around for about five minutes, then flew straight up into the sky. They also claim that the lights were "bright orange" and "strangely shaped", and changed colour, from green to yellow to white to orange. These UFOs visited the family three times on October 26th, 2009, and, as a result, left the family so disturbed and upset that they decided to contact the Ministry of Defence in the hope that they could help them.

The MoD responded by saying they only investigate sightings where there is a significant threat to the UK as a whole from an external source, and that as no such evidence regarding UFOs had been submitted yet, there was therefore nothing they could do.

The MoD's UFO desk was closed in 2009, after they decided that investigations into UFO sightings served no real

UK UFOs

purpose, but merely diverted air defence specialists from their main tasks. However, some UFO experts questioned this decision, fearing that the closure would leave British airspace open to attack and witnesses forced to depend on the media and UFO experts to investigate their reports of possible UFO sightings.

Chapter Eleven: UFOs Over London

On a typical New Year's Eve, we all know how much the sky becomes illuminated by all sorts of fireworks and Chinese lanterns amid the celebrations. However, on one particular Hogmany that marked the end of 2014, a light was seen in the sky over London that definitely did not seem to be one of the conventional kind.

Revellers spotted this weird greenish object hovering above the London Eye during the BBC coverage of the New Year celebrations. Although some thought it might be Chinese lantern, which are always popular at New Year along with the fireworks, this UFO appeared to fly in a very unusual arc from behind the London tourist attraction, before flying towards the opposite side of the River Thames.

When the footage was posted on YouTube, it generated mass speculation on whether or not the strange light really was an alien spacecraft. Some thought it was just a camera drone, while others pointed out that the light was much too conspicuous and attention-catching, amid all the fireworks going off all around it, to be a drone. One YouTube user commented that it was not unusual for flying saucers to be curious about our lights and electricity.

In another YouTube UFO clip, captured on 25th May 2014, a video seems to show a UFO in the skies over London. The video was filmed from the window of an aircraft. The clip, two minutes and five seconds in duration, shows a strange dark-coloured disc sporting lights on either side of its body. The object seems to flying above the line of clouds.

Since being posted on YouTube, the UFO video has had over 92,000 views. As is usual with such clips, both the believers and the sceptics have argued for and against the video's authenticity. One viewer dismissed the footage as just a trick manufactured by a clever Photoshop user. Another, like a lot of sceptics, thought it was a military drone of some kind.

Staying with YouTube, on 23rd December 2014, a video was posted there by an organisation called UFO Watch UK. Named the "Group of White Orb UFOs Over West London", the video appears to show just that: an unidentified group of white objects hovering in the capital's skies. Some experts who have analysed the video opine that the white objects are perhaps birds in flight or drones buzzing around. On the other hand, there are also a lot of people who think that this footage is definite evidence of a group of UFOs flying over London.

On 26th June 2011, a YouTube user filmed what he believed to be a UFO flying at high altitude over London, near the BBC Radio 1 building in Great Portland Street. The video shows specks of white light – possibly from an alien spacecraft or some other unidentified source. A larger object then appears from behind a cloud, then disappears a few seconds later. The same user shot another video of the strange object from inside the offices of a visual effects company. One the same day, there were also other reports of strange UFO sightings near the Tower Bridge area, some of which can be viewed on YouTube.

Author's Note

If you enjoyed this book, I would really appreciate it if you could leave a review for it on Amazon.

You can also join the Facebook UK UFOs group.

Feel free also to check out my Amazon Author Page.

Alan Toner
www.wirralwriter.co.uk
www.trueghoststories.co.uk

Twitter Profile: Scouselad8
Facebook Profile: mersey.male1

Printed in Great Britain
by Amazon